Finding the Pain in your @ss-umption

A Leadership Tale

by Matt Rawlins Ph.D.

Green Bench Consulting Pte. Ltd
Amuzement Publications

Cover design by Kelvin Marc Tan - Thank you.
Editing by Pateenah Hordern, Fiona Gifford & Aimee
Rawlins - Thank you.
Art work by Ron Reiman - Thank you.

Published by Green Bench Consulting Pte. Ltd. /
Amuzement Publications

Finding the pain in your @ss-umption by Matt Rawlins.
Copyright © 2012 Matt Rawlins.

ISBN # 1-928715-12-5

OTHER LEADERSHIP BOOKS
BY MATT RAWLINS

The Green Bench
A dialogue about Leadership & Change

The Green Bench II
Ongoing dialogue about Leadership & Communication

There's an Elephant in the Room
Discover the single most powerful tool for growth

The Lottery
A question can change a life

These titles are available in iBooks and Kindle formats.

Most of our assumptions have
outlived their uselessness.
Marshall McLuhan

Begin challenging your own
assumptions. Your assumptions
are your windows on the world.
Scrub them off every once in awhile,
or the light won't come in.
Alan Alda

Table of Contents

Welcome

Imagine a relationship without conflict…

As much as we would like to, we can't. Conflict is actually an important part of our relationships and woven into the very fabric of our lives.

Whether we like it or not, how you and I deal with conflict, will determine who we are and in the end the quality of the life we enjoy with others.

In this leadership tale, you will discover that the real and very hard work of dealing with conflict is not really about a donkey or a game at all, but about the @ss-umptions we make and the challenge of being willing to expose and then deal with those @sses in our life.

Please bear with me as there are a few times I leave the word @ss a bit vague. It can be an aggressive word with meanings that includes, being foolish, shifting the blame, being vulnerable or just a provocative way of dealing with an @ss-umption, in general. I have done this to get you to think about the challenges of dealing with conflict. As conflict seems to include all those meanings above.

That being said, let the tale begin…

Once upon a time, in a not so far away land, there was a company that was struggling with creativity, communication and keeping up with a changing world. This company realized they were in trouble and didn't know what to do about it.

They found an Instructor who had the audacity to tell them that he could teach anyone how to learn about the conflict in these 3 areas in a simple game of "Pin the tail on the donkey'.

So this company found two employees who seemed to represent what they struggled with most and sent them off as volunteers.

Scooter was shy and reluctant. He avoided conflict whenever he possibly could and did what was expected of him. He fit in well with others and didn't cause any waves.

Boomer was confident and aggressive. He moved towards conflict and had strong opinions on everything. He was used to getting his way and wasn't afraid to bend others to his will.

Neither of these two were particularly good at games. They were also very different in how they approached this game and dare I say... even their lives. But in the end, the Instructor was right. What Scooter and Boomer learned gave them tools to be more creative, communicate better and deal more effectively with a changing world.

Lesson 1

Pin the tail on the Donkey

The Instructor welcomed them and introductions were made. Boomer and Scooter quickly understood the goal of the game.

"All you have to do is pin this tail on that picture of a Donkey?" Scooter repeated quietly as the Instructor gave them instructions.

"In essence, yes, there will be a few variations along the way, but that is it. Are you ready?" the Instructor asked.

Both agreed and the game began.

Boomer quickly walked over and reached out to grab the tail that was in the

Instructor's hand. He had other things to do and wanted to get it over with as quickly as possible.

The Instructor held the tail away and said, "Thank you for volunteering first Boomer. Let me help you."

The Instructor pulled out a blindfold and held it up for Boomer to put on.

Boomer stared at it like it was a virus being offered him. The Instructor reached up and put the blindfold on Boomer.

Boomer declared, "Hey, I can't see anything with this stupid thing on."

"That is the point of having it on. Now I am going to turn you around so relax and let me help you," the Instructor said calmly. He then took Boomer by the shoulders and began to turn him in a circle.

After one turn around Boomer reached up and ripped the blindfold off his eyes and stared at the Instructor. After a moment he was able to focus and questioned, "What are you doing? I won't even be able to stand if you keep that up."

Boomer turned and walked carefully over and sat down. He then turned to Scooter and declared, "You go first."

Boomer had decided a long time ago that anything you did, you attacked. You took control and won by sheer power. He was completely thrown off when he lost his sense of power and thus control.

Scooter was glued to his seat, he was not used to being the first to try something. The risk was too great. The Instructor walked over and gently pulled Scooter up. As Scooter was used to doing what others wanted, he tried to resist, but it was useless. He quickly found himself standing next to the Instructor who held out the blindfold for him to put on. He reluctantly put it on and braced himself. The Instructor slowly began to spin him around.

Within a few turns he was completely disorientated. When the Instructor stopped turning him he just stood there. He had no sense of where the donkey was and was completely off-balance.

Truth be told, he was not that uncomfortable with being disorientated. It seemed he lived a good portion of his life that way. What was very uncomfortable for him was to have to make a decision on his own preferences with no help. He knew he was supposed to find the donkey but that was not possible. A sense of responsibility, the weight to do what was 'right', the fear of failure all seemed to paralyze him.

Finally the Instructor reached up and took off the blindfold as it was obvious Scooter was not going to move.

Scooter looked around for a moment and quickly got his sense back and walked over sat down.

The two students just sat there and said nothing for two very different reasons.

The Instructor stated, "I guess that will be the end of the first lesson. In this game, you are going to be disorientated. That is a part of the game and if you don't learn to accept it, you will never be able to succeed at this game."

Boomer left angry.
Scooter left intrigued.

Disequilibrium
is a normal part
of conflict.

Lesson 2

Boomer and Scooter sat in their chairs as the Instructor walked into the room.

Boomer looked confident. He also looked tired like he had been up most of the night trying to figure it all out.

Scooter looked refreshed as he slept really good. It was just another day.

"Boomer, you look like you are ready for this. Come on up," the Instructor began.

Boomer rose up and walked up to the Instructor confidently. He grabbed the blindfold and put it on and stood there with his hand pointing at the last place he had seen the donkey before he put on his blindfold.

The Instructor started to slowly turn Boomer in a cirle. He also grabbed his hand that was still pointed at the picture of the donkey on the wall and moved it up and down and back and forth.

You could see an angry look on Boomers face growing stronger. Finally he stopped spinning and the Instructor said, "Okay, pin the tail on the donkey.

Boomer somewhat confidently walked over to the wall and put the tail on the wall. He then tore off his blindfold and looked at where he pinned the tail and it was five feet away from the donkey. Boomer quickly walked over, unpinned the picture of the donkey and moved it right next to the tail.

He then turned and faced Scooter who had a wide-eyed stare on his face and Scooter quickly looked down at the ground. Boomer then turned to the Instructor and tried to intimidate him.

The Instructor smiled and walked over and quietly unpinned the picture and moved it back. He looked at Boomer and just smiled. He said nothing but was not intimidated at all.

Boomer strode over and sat down hard on the chair. He then glared at Scooter who was still staring at the floor and who had no desire to look over at Boomer.

"Scooter, your turn," the Instructor called out.

Scooter quickly rose up to try and get as much distance from Boomer as he could. He took one last look at the image of the donkey and held it clearly in his mind and then quickly put on the blindfold and stood waiting to be turned around.

As he turned around, he didn't focus on his disequilibrium but kept the picture in his mind of what he wanted. He pictured where it was and slowly began to move toward it. He then pinned the tail on the wall and stood there for a second. Slowly he took his blindfold off and had actually pinned it only 6 inches away from the end of the donkey.

"Well done," the Instructor called out.

Scooter just smiled, a bit embarrassed at his success. He didn't dare turn and look at Boomer, as that was not even an option.

Visualize what you
want. Keep it clear
in your mind.
(Ignore the
disequilibrium)

Lesson 3

Boomer and Scooter made it to class on time and were ready for the new day.

Boomer had worked hard on a new strategy to give him the confidence to win, which he so desired. He stood up when the Instructor offered and walked forward. He took the blindfold and put it on and just before he did, he got his feet set up the way he practiced last night.

The Instructor turned him around and could see him counting his steps as he tried carefully to move them in a certain way. Just as Boomer was getting ready to move toward the donkey, the Instructor reversed the way he was turning him and turned him around the opposite way for a couple turns.

Boomer was getting that angry look on his face but tried to step out confidently and put the tail on the wall. He then lifted his blindfold off and realized he was 4 feet off on the other side.

He turned and glared at the Instructor and vented, "You switched the way you turned me. It's not fair, I had it all figured out and you switched on me. How can I do this if you don't play fair. It's all your fault I didn't get as close today."

The Instructor smiled and replied, "No conflict is ever exactly the same. Each conflict is different and you have to be prepared for that. You think a technique is going to give you certainty, to make you 'right', sorry but it doesn't work that way."

Scooter stood up quickly and avoided Boomer. He stood there for a moment with the tail in his one hand and the blindfold in his other. A smile broke out on his face.

The Instructor asked, "What is the smile for?"

Scooter looked over at Boomer who was working on his strategy to count steps and fully preoccupied with himself, so he said in a soft voice, "I was also thinking about the blind fold. This is great. It's like it gives permission to not know and then I can be curious. I mean how can I know when I am blindfolded?"

Scooter slid the blindfold on and was turned around in circles both ways and then stood still for a moment to focus. He walked over and pinned the tail on the wall and then slid his blindfold off. He was six inches above the mark.

Scooter quietly went and sat down. Boomer didn't even notice Scooter, as he was still busy trying to perfect his step technique.

Each conflict is a
unique opportunity.
You can't know
everything.
Get curious, it helps
you find the @ss.

Lesson 4

Boomer had spent much of the night working on his new 'dual turn' strategy and was prepared today for either turn. As he walked into the class he saw a live donkey standing patiently next to the Instructor.

He gave a loud 'humph' and went over and sat down. Scooter came in with an excited look on his face and when he saw the donkey, his grin widened. He reluctantly sat down next to a fuming Boomer.

The Instructor smiled at them both, "Welcome to the game. We have a bit of a twist on the game and I trust you will find it an opportunity to learn some new things. Who wants to go first?"

Boomer and Scooter sat there in silence for a moment not daring to look at the Instructor.

Finally the Instructor responded, "Hmm, a bit intimidated are we? Scooter, how about you taking the first attempt?"

Scooter, wanting to please the Instructor, reluctantly stood up and shuffled over to him. The Instructor walked the donkey over to a post set up on the wall and tied the donkey to it and walked back to where Scooter stood.

"I heard they kick," Scooter mumbled to the Instructor.

"They have a pretty good kick," the Instructor replied as he handed Scooter a rope with Velcro on the end. "This little lady is pretty tame and it's pretty rare that she kicks. The key is, treat her with respect and she will treat you right. Just attach the end of the rope to the spot on her tail that I have attached the other side of the Velcro."

Scooter put on the blindfold and held the rope in his hand. He was turned around a few times and stood there. Now the problem was not where was the donkey, but how to deal with the donkey. That seemed like a very different and much more challenging task.

Scooter shuffled forward, fearing each step he was going to be kicked across the room. He could hear the donkey breathing and continued to move closer. He gathered all his strength and reached out his hand and felt the hair and pushed a bit and quickly let go and took a step back.

He quickly pulled the blindfold off and took another step back. He saw the rope on the floor by the donkeys back leg and realized he was closer than he really wanted to be, but he was safe. Nothing had happened to him. He walked over to the chair and sat down with a sense of relief.

The Instructor pointed to Boomer who had gone stone cold. He was glaring back at the Instructor, but to no avail. He got up and walked over and tried staring at the donkey who turned and looked at him for a moment and then turned away.

Boomer walked over to the corner and picked up a leg of a chair that must have broken off and been set there. He walked back over to the Instructor. As he stood there the donkey turned and looked at him and then brayed out loud.

The Instructor reached over and gently pried the leg out of Boomers hand and said, "She's aware of your fear."

"I am not afraid of that donkey," Boomer quickly declared.

"She senses it," the Instructor stated.

Boomer quickly decided this conversation was not going where he wanted it to go and put on his blindfold. The Instructor turned him around and then switched him around again and then stopped him.

Boomer didn't even bother to count his steps, as he knew where the donkey was. It wasn't some abstract picture he was dealing with. He was dealing with a smelly, dirty, stupid, living and possible kicking donkey.

He slowly edged toward the donkey. He held the rope in his hand more like a whip than a tail to be pinned on it. When he was close, he thrust out his hand and at the same instant the donkey brayed and kicked the air right next to where Boomer was standing.

Boomer jumped back and ripped the blindfold off his face and began to swear. He turned to the Instructor and declared, "You said she didn't kick. Are you wanting a fight?"

The Instructor held up both his hands and responded, "I said it's rare that she does. She could sense your willingness to hurt her and responded."

"I am not dealing with that @ss any more. She is dangerous and I am not going near her without some protection."

Boomer just couldn't get it through his head that he played any part in the donkey's response. He couldn't see that he was reacting to the donkey out of his own fear. The truth was, to even admit that he had fears, was more than he could bear.

He was so used to getting and having the power and dominating others that when matched with a situation where he had no power, he didn't want any involvement at all.

Boomer turned and walked over to his seat and it looked like he was going to kick Scooter but at the last instant, kicked the chair next to him and yelled out, "That stupid @ss almost kicked me."

In that moment, time seemed to slow down for Scooter as he listened to Boomer's words and watched him do just what he was mad at the donkey for doing.

Somehow it all came together in this idea, *'Whose the @ss now?'* Then, another thought came to him. *'He can't see it but his @ss-umptions about dealing with the donkey was the problem.'* Then finally the thought came crystal clear, *'the @ss-umption is the real problem here.'*

Scooter chuckled out loud at the last thought.

Boomer turned to him and demanded, "What you laughing at? Do you have a problem?"

Scooter quickly wiped the smile off his face and responded, "No, I am not laughing at this, it just reminded me of something Boomer. Sorry, I didn't mean to offend you."

The Instructor quickly walked over and said, "Looks like that is enough class work for today. Let's pick it up from here tomorrow."

Scooter got up quickly and left while Boomer sat fuming.

The problem is not conflict, it can be healthy.
It is the undealt with @ss-umptions in it that cause the conflict.

Lesson 5

Scooter walked into the class and was surprised to see Boomer sitting there. He didn't think he would come anymore. This game didn't seem to fit him very well.

Scooter sat down and the Instructor walked in and welcomed them.

Boomer stated, "Just so you know, I am not playing the game anymore. I am just an observer. I will watch and learn, but I am not playing till I figure it out."

"Your choice I guess, but you can't figure it out without playing it. There is a risk involved, always. And you don't have any risk sitting there," the Instructor replied.

"My choice. I will just watch. Just teach him," pointing to Scooter, "and I will learn from my seat," Boomer replied.

Boomer @ss-umed that life was too painful and certainty was the only way to protect himself. He needed to be right. To have the right technique that would give him the safety he so desired. He figured he could watch Scooter make all the mistakes and be the fool and then he could get it right and not be the fool. It made complete sense to him because of his @ss-umptions.

Scooter had spent a lot of time thinking about the last class. Listening to Boomer and the Instructors conversation and watching their body language seemed to make it all clearer for him, Boomers @ss-umption was the problem. He couldn't see that he was making @ss-umptions about the game, about himself and his relationships. Those @sses were the source of the problem in learning the game and thus dealing with conflict.

The Instructor walked over to them and said, "Now, Boomer, you can't say anything or make any noises. Is that clear?"

Boomer nodded and the Instructor came over to Scooter and patted him on his back and said, "A new twist, as I am sure you can see things have changed and our donkey friend is not here. I have hidden a small picture of a donkey and you need to find it."

"No blindfold?" Scooter asked.

"No, you need your eyes. Donkeys come in all sizes and shapes. You will need to search hard to find it as it will be difficult to find but I can assure you it is in plain sight."

Scooter stood up and looked around the room, wondering where to start. He picked a corner and walked over there and starting looking in and around the books and chairs. After a short while, he heard Boomer snickering as he looked. He kept on looking and tried to ignore him but it became harder and harder to ignore him as he just had a big, mocking grin on his face and the body language spoke loud and clear as he shifted in his seat.

The harder he tried to ignore Boomer, the less he could. He continued his looking around now in a half-hearted way but was soon ready to give up. It was as if he himself was being kicked by the donkey today.

He stood up and looked around the room with a slow glance. He turned his head and his eye caught the mirror which reflected an image of his back. He stared for a moment and realized that on his back was an image of a donkey. He lifted his arm over his shoulder and pulled off the small image of the donkey that was taped to his back.

He stated to the Instructor, "You put it on me when you patted me on the back!"

"Donkeys are usually in the place you are least likely to look," the Instructor replied.

Scooter was struck by the same thought that hit him yesterday; My @ss-umption is the problem. I @ss-umed it was in a certain place and never questioned the @ss.

Boomer wasn't laughing at me, but at my @ss-umption. I don't need to take it personally.

Scooter began to think about pain and of being vulnerable. He had taken the risk to play the game. He exposed his @ss–umptions and it hurt, especially when he was being laughed at and mocked by Boomer. He was tempted to blame Boomer and then realized that would be no different than Boomer blaming the donkey yesterday for his problems. It would be an easy way to escape facing the pain of the risk, but then he would be a victim and what was the @ss-umption associated with that? He could sit and be safe and watch others take risk and expose their @ss and they would learn and grow, or he could experience life for himself. He realized it was no easy choice to take a risk and expose your @ss-umptions.

The Instructor stood quietly and watched Scooter in deep thought. Finally he said, "Looks like we all have something to think about."

Boomer stood and stated as he walked out, "I love watching this game. It is great!"

Scooter slowly walked out as his mind was working overtime to try and hold all that was going on inside of him.

To find the @ss-umptions, you must learn to ask questions as they are usually very hard to find.

Dealing with your @ss-umptions always requires a risk.

Conflict doesn't make
you an @ss.
It just exposes your
@ss-umption. If you are
willing, you can learn a
lot from conflict.

It's your choice!

Lesson 6

Scooter walked into the class and there sat Boomer with a big smile on his face, waiting for the day's entertainment.

"Welcome Scooter, glad you could make it," the Instructor stated when he saw Scooter.

"Thank you, I was actually looking forward to the time." He turned and looked at Boomer and continued, "Most of it anyway."

The Instructor walked over and handed a blank piece of paper with some color pencils to Scooter, "Here, I want you to draw the donkey this morning. I want you to be really careful, take your time and make it an expression of yourself."

The Instructor turned to Boomer and said, "What do you think Boomer? You want to take a shot at creating your own donkey? You can't fail as it is your donkey."

Boomer replied, "If you give me a picture to copy, I would give it a try, but this whole thing as an 'expression of myself' and 'it is your donkey' is a bit crazy. A donkey is just a donkey. No thanks, I prefer to just watch."

Scooter turned his back to Boomer and just sat thinking for a while. Then slowly began to draw. The Instructor pulled out a book and began to read. Boomer kept trying to see Scooters work but Scooter had it well guarded.

An hour passed and finally Scooter held up his drawing to the Instructor who came over and looked at it. Boomer also jumped up and looked at it as well.

"That is good Scooter, you are actually an artist. You have a good sense of humor as well. I love the big smile you put on it."

Boomer reached out and picked it up to look at it more closely. Suddenly, he raised his head back and opened his mouth and sneezed right into the picture of the donkey. He then held the paper by the edge and gave it back to Scooter who was in shock at what just happened.

Boomer broke out laughing and turned to sit down and the Instructor glared at Boomer but then looked to Scooter.

Scooter looked at the Instructor who had his eyes engaged on him, waiting to see what he would do. His eyes were like an invitation to use this as a part of the game.

Scooter knew then he had a choice. What would he do with this?

He had invested time and energy to make that picture a part of himself, and expression of what he liked. The picture was important to him. The donkey was important to him. The @ss was an expression of himself. It was his @ss-umption…

Then it hit him.

If you take care of an @ss-umpton.

If you nurture it, watch out for it and feed it.

If it is an expression of yourself, then it is really hard to deal with an attack on it or it's loss.

Scooter's mind continued to work. He thought of how people often get @ss-umptions that end up defining us:

Your family gives you @ss-umptions about who you are as you grow up. It feels like so much a part of you that you can't see it or even recognize it as an @ss.

He thought of fights that he had with people from different cultures. How he judged them and mocked them. Yet all he was doing was exposing his @ss-umptions. Culture was simply a safe place, where a group agreed upon certain @ss-umptions and no one questioned them or exposed them.

Scooter turned and faced Boomer and for the first time in his life, realized that he didn't have to fear him. That even though he had operated by some bad

@ss-umptions, he could learn something from him about his own painful @ss-umptions and in a strange way it would help him to grow.

Boomer sat there and just glared at them, daring them to say or do something.

The Instructor stated, "I guess we know who the real donkey was this morning. You played your part well and you were not hard to find. It seems like we could almost say thank you, but I don't think that is appropriate."

With that, the class ended for the day.

Scooter's challenge became clear: *I have been running from conflict my whole life. In actuality, I have been running from myself my whole life because of some core @ss-umptions I have in me and I didn't like how conflict exposed my @ss.*

He realized he lived by this motto: *Better to protect my @ss and run then face the pain of dealing with a bad @ss.*

An @ss~umption is a
very personal thing.
Treat it with respect.
Remember, someone
has invested a part
of their life in it
and will go to great
lengths to defend it.

Lesson 7

Scooter walked into the class and was the first one there. He wasn't sure if he was relieved or disappointed that Boomer wasn't there. Before he could decide, Boomer walked in and sat down. Scooter was amazed at how he could say so much without using a word. It was like his very presence mocked him.

Before he could think about it any more, he knew there was a painfully bad @ss-umption in that thought somewhere; the Instructor came in with the donkey again on a halter.

Boomer got serious quickly and scooted his chair back away.

The Instructor began, "As you can see, I brought our friend with me to help us today."

As they settled in the Instructor continued, "Truth be told, I needed some help carrying heavy boxes of books to another classroom and thought Pepper, that's her name, could help us."

The Instructor pulled out a rope carrier to fit over the saddle and fitted her with it while Scooter and Boomer put the boxes carefully in their place on her back.

Boomer asked with a twisted smile, "Can I take the reign and lead Pepper?"

Just then Pepper brayed loudly. The Instructor replied, "I don't think she would do much for you Boomer. She works by trust and I don't think you have that relationship yet."

With that, they began to move the books. After several trips they had moved all the books and were heading back to the classroom when Pepper lifted her tail and crapped on the floor.

The Instructor stated in frustration, "I knew I should have got her outside quicker, but I thought we could get those last boxes in before she needed to do her duty. Scooter, can you and Boomer clean that up for me?"

Boomer pinched his nose and stated, "I can't stand the smell. I will puke soon if I don't get out of here." And off he fled.

Scooter replied, "Sure, I can clean this up."

As he walked off to find some kind of a shovel the Instructor replied, "Careful, you might learn something," and walked off with Pepper.

A shovel was soon found with some paper towels and the mess was quickly taken care of. Scooter reflected on the mess and if you saw him cleaning it up you would have been amazed to see the smile on his face as his little mind was at work learning all he could in this little 'game'.

He quickly figured out that the @ss was a huge help carrying the books, that if it was agreed upon and fit the purpose of what they were trying to do, @ss-umptions were a vital part of life.

He was also aware that all @sses have the capacity to make a mess and that is a normal expression of an @ss.

Clarify and work with
@ss-umptions as
they can
be a great help.

Remember all @ss-umptions
can make a mess. That is a
part of their very nature.

Scooter and Boomer walked into the class at the same time. The Instructor was already there.

"Welcome to the class," the Instructor said as they walked in. He looked over at them and then continued on, "I have hidden several images of donkeys in the room. See if you can find them. Boomer, you want to try and look?"

"Ugh, sure, why not. How hard can that be?" Boomer replied as he stood up to look around.

Scooter stood up and didn't move but just looked slowly around the room. He discreetly checked his back and there was nothing there so he began his search.

After a half hour or so Boomer declared, "There are no donkeys here. You just enjoy mocking us." With that he walked over and sat down.

Scooter watched Boomer sit down and stood still and reflected. He looked at his Instructor who had a curious look on his face. This time he thought about the words the Instructor used and what he @ss-umed he meant. Then thought, '*Question my @ss-umption.*'

He slowly looked around the room. He saw a piece of paper he quickly passed over before and went back and looked at it. There was a faint image of something on it but it was not a clear image. He questioned his @ss-umption, What could an image of a donkey look like?

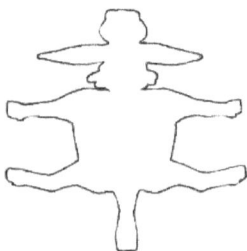

Then out of nowhere, the image of the donkey popped out at Scooter. It was a picture from above, looking down at a donkey that was flattened.

He continued his search and found four small hooves on a paper. It was a picture of a donkey looking up at it from below.

Another picture of what could only be a close up of a nose of a donkey.

A short while later Scooter brought his collection of images over to the Instructor and showed them to him while he explained his thinking.

Boomer was curious, he stood up and quickly walked over to listen to Scooter explain what he found to the Instructor.

The Instructor smiled and nodded in agreement as Scooter shared. He finally said, "Well done."

Boomer declared, "That's not fair. You said images of donkeys and these are not like the other images you showed us. You tricked us again. You seem to enjoy that. Mocking us and making us look like an @ss."

"That's your @ss-umption, I only said images of donkeys. I didn't say what parts or how you would see them. You @ss-umed that but it was not what I meant? If you had questioned me I would have been glad to give you extra information to help you," the Instructor replied.

Scooter thought about it.

'Question the meaning of words and images you @ss-ume to be true.
Words are made up of meanings.
Meanings have an @ss-umption in them.'

@sses are not stupid. But the person using the @ss in a wrong way sure can be.

Boomer and Scooter sat in the class as the Instructor walked in holding two strings that were attached to balloons floating behind him.

The Instructor began, "Welcome to the last class. Today will be a bit different."

"Each class is totally different! What is he talking about?" Boomer commented loud enough for Scooter to hear him.

Scooter glanced over at him and then looked back at the Instructor who continued, "Okay, here is the game today." The Instructor walked over and gave each of them a balloon and a felt pen. Boomer reluctantly took it.

"You need to play today Boomer as it needs two people. First I want you to draw a picture of a donkey on your balloon. It doesn't have to be fancy, but just draw your donkey on the balloon. And be careful not to pop it, please."

Boomer and Scooter held the balloon between their legs and quickly drew a picture of a donkey on it. When they finished the Instructor took their pen and gave them a needle. Each of them took it carefully.

"Good, now both please stand up and put a little distance between you."

Scooter took a couple of steps away and Boomer took one small one.

"Okay, the game is very simple. The goal is to try and pop the other balloon while protecting yours." A look of concern came over Scooters face and a smile came over Boomers.

As they started to move around the Instructor quickly added, "You cannot poke the other person with the needle. If you do, you automatically lose."

Boomer then lost his smile for a brief second and Scooter sighed with a slight relief and the game began.

Boomer and Scooter stood looking at each other for a second. Boomer put his hand with the balloon behind him and started to move toward Scooter.

Scooter hesitated for a moment and then put his hand holding the balloon behind him. He backed up a step and looked intently at Boomer.

They slowly circled each other and Boomer stepped in quickly and swung his hand with the needle at the balloon. Scooter quickly turned from him and stepped back.

They went around in circles for several minutes as they tried to get behind the other person and get at the @ss (balloon) while protecting their own @ss (balloon).

Just as Boomer was getting more aggressive and trying to attack more the Instructor called out, "Time is up. Now step back and I want you to think for a second, as you were playing that game what where you thinking or feeling while it was going on?"

As Scooter was deep in thought, Boomer slipped behind him and popped Scooters balloon. As a loud 'BANG' filled the room and Scooter jumped, Boomer smiled and looked at the Instructor and stated, "I was thinking about winning. Defending my balloon and trying to attack him. To find a way to catch him off balance."

As Boomer was talking, Scooter slipped over next to Boomer and popped his balloon as he finished talking. A loud 'BANG' filled the room again. Boomer turned to stare down Scooter who just smiled in return and stated, "I was thinking the same thing."

The Instructor stood silent for a moment and then said, "Okay, good. I am glad that is clear. Let me summarize our time together as we wrap up the class and say this, 'It is this mentality, perspective, focus or paradigm that you just talked about,

I have been working with you on this whole time. The problem is when you view conflict as a competition. When it is something to be won, with a winner and a loser. When the focus is solely on trying to outwit, gather power and beat the other person while defending yourself. This is the core challenge in any conflict you are dealing with. Simply put, you try and expose his @ss while protecting your own @ss.'"

Boomer stood for the first time and actually thought about what the Instructor had said as it seemed so clear to him that this was the only way he dealt with any conflict in life. To have another way of viewing it was a completely new thought that had never entered his mind.

Scooter smiled as the words settled into his thinking. This was a great way to summarize the struggle he felt. He would rarely attack but he could see how he was being defensive by not talking about or even being willing to deal with the @ss-umptions involved in the conflict. He could see Boomer became defensive by attacking. Scooter saw that he became defensive by hiding in the expectations of others. And he saw clearly that if you were not dealing with the @ss-umptions, you were not dealing with the conflict. He had so much to learn and it was no small challenge to not be defensive all the time.

The Instructor walked over and shook their hands, "Congratulations, I know it has been a bit of a challenge, but I think you are beginning to look at conflict in a new way. I would encourage you to continue to think about it and explore different ways to communicate that allow you to deal with the @ss-umptions involved in the conflict. I can assure you that if you just do this some of the time, you will see remarkable results in working with people."

Boomer sat for a moment and thought about the exercise as if hearing some foreign language that might make sense for the first time in his life. In his way of thinking, dealing with conflict was pure and simply about 'Power' and 'Control'.

Maybe, just maybe, there were times when this @ss-umption was the problem, not the answer.

To defend your @ss and attack someone else's @ss will only escalate conflict.

With this mentality, in the long term, there are no winners. Just victors and enemies.

The End

And that my friend is the end of this leadership tale.

You and I are left with the dilemma of when to protect our @ss and when not to. If you are like the rest of us, I can say that you over protect it and rarely expose it for what it is.

Want something new for your life? Then an important part of the answer is in your @ss-umptions.

Remember, you can't save your face and your @ss-umption at the same time.

Instructor's Notes

Scooter and Boomer's challenge is our challenge. They protect their @ss-umptions when threatened. They do this in different ways. We all have a little of each in us.

Scooter	Boomer
Withdraw	Attack
Don't take Risk	Risk only when Right / Argue you are always right
Declare you have no agenda	Keep agenda hidden
Accept Responsibility / Do only what you are responsible for	Seek Power
Deny Feelings	Deny Feelings
Avoid Conflicts	Win all conflicts
Silence	Blame others
Goal = Safe by not getting involved or doing only what is expected	Goal = Safe by being in Control over others through power
Avoid exposing your @ss-umptions	Avoid exposing your @ss-umptions

Conflict always creates disequilibrium.

Focus on what you want, not on the disequilibrium.

The problem is not
conflict, it can be
healthy.

It is the undealt
with @ss-umptions in it
that cause the conflict.

**Clarify and work with
@ss-umptions and they
can be a great help.**

**Remember
all @ss-umptions can
make a mess. That is a
part of their very nature.**

Conflict doesn't make
you an @ss.
It just exposes
your @ss-umptions.

If you are willing,
You can learn a lot
from conflict.

It's your choice.

An @ss-umption is a very personal thing.

Treat it with respect.

Remember, someone has invested a part of their life in it and will go to great lengths to defend it.

Pick any conflict you
are involved in.

You can be assured
of this;

There are some bad
@sses involved in it.

Question is: Do you have
the courage to be vulner-
able enough to find them
and deal with them?

All conflict involves a risk.

Risks make us feel vulnerable.

We hate being vulnerable.
-therefore-
We avoid conflict.

Where is the @ss
-umption in this?

@sses are not stupid.

But the person
using the @ss
in a wrong way
in a wrong way
sure can be.

When you are dealing with conflict you can be assured of this;

You are always dealing with a Pain in your @ss.

Perhaps a better way of
saying it;

Dealing with @ss-umptions
is at the heart of
resolving conflict.

It requires vulnerability
and possible pain.

Give yourself and others
the freedom to work with
different @ss-umptions.

But at least have the integrity
to talk about the @ss-umptions
so you know what is really
going on.

About the Author

Unabashed in his pointed questions and unrelenting in his encouragement for those around him to live a life of integrity, Dr. Matthew Rawlins is a passionate educator and brilliant communicator in both speech and writing. He has been invited to lecture in over 25 nations, and has published 11 books. He gained his Ph.D. in communication and leadership development through the University of Wales, and currently is CEO of Green Bench Consulting in Singapore. His work focuses on executive coaching as well as difficult conversations in organizational change, leadership, and conflict.

If you are interested in bulk orders of this book, posters or have questions, you can contact Matt Rawlins.

Email: mrawlins@mac.com
Company website is: thegreenbench.com
Facebook: Green Bench Consulting